Dinosaur Graveyards in Africa

by Grace Hansen

Abdo Kids Jumbo is an Imprint of Abdo Kids
abdobooks.com

abdobooks.com

Published by Abdo Kids, a division of ABDO, P.O. Box 398166, Minneapolis, Minnesota 55439.
Copyright © 2022 by Abdo Consulting Group, Inc. International copyrights reserved in all countries.
No part of this book may be reproduced in any form without written permission from the publisher.
Abdo Kids Jumbo™ is a trademark and logo of Abdo Kids.

Printed in the United States of America, North Mankato, Minnesota.

102021

012022

THIS BOOK CONTAINS
RECYCLED MATERIALS

Photo Credits: Alamy, AP Images, Getty Images, iStock, Science Source, Shutterstock,
©Paul C. Sereno p21 / CC BY 3.0, ©Masato Hattori p20-21

Production Contributors: Teddy Borth, Jennie Forsberg, Grace Hansen
Design Contributors: Candice Keimig, Pakou Moua

Library of Congress Control Number: 2021940117
Publisher's Cataloging-in-Publication Data

Names: Hansen, Grace, author.

Title: Dinosaur graveyards in Africa / by Grace Hansen

Description: Minneapolis, Minnesota : Abdo Kids, 2022 | Series: Dinosaur graveyards | Includes online
    resources and index.

Identifiers: ISBN 9781098209445 (lib. bdg.) | ISBN 9781098260156 (ebook) | ISBN 9781098260507
    (Read-to-Me ebook)

Subjects: LCSH: Dinosaurs--Juvenile literature. | Fossils--Juvenile literature. | Africa--Juvenile literature. |
    Paleontology--Juvenile literature. | Paleontological excavations--Juvenile literature.

Classification: DDC 567--dc23

Table of Contents

Dinosaurs of Africa

Dinosaurs lived between 245 and 66 million years ago. After a dinosaur's death, its remains could turn to fossil if the conditions were right. This process takes more than 10,000 years!

Every continent has dinosaur fossils, including Africa. Fossils are often found in **rock formations**. Some formations hold more remains than others!

Europe
Asia
Africa
N
W
E
S

Tendaguru Formation

The Tendaguru Formation is in Tanzania. Many dinosaur fossils are buried there. Some belong to large sauropods that once roamed the area.

Giraffatitan
• Sauropod
• Late Jurassic
• Herbivore
• Nearly as long as 2 school buses
Giraffatitan hindlimb
Africa
Tanzania
N
S
E
W
9

Kentrosaurus fossils were discovered in many of the formation's quarries.

Kentrosaurus

• Stegosaurian

• Late Jurassic

• Herbivore

• Name means
"Sharp-point lizard"

Kentrosaurus
display

Bahariya Formation

Some of the largest dinosaur species have been dug up in Egypt's Bahariya Formation. Paralititan was a giant sauropod! A **partial** skeleton was found in 1999.

Paralititan

- **Titanosaurian sauropod**

- **Late Cretaceous**

- **Herbivore**

- **As long as a Boeing 737-500 airplane**

Spinosaurus fossils were also found in the formation. This dinosaur was the largest meat-eater to ever live!

Spinosaurus
Theropod
Late Cretaceous
Carnivore
As long as a semi-trailer
Spinosaurus teeth

Kem Kem Beds

The Kem Kem Beds of Morocco
are filled with fossils. Rugops
remains were discovered there.
Many **Pterosaur** species were
found there too.

Alanqa
• Pterosaur
• Late Cretaceous
• Carnivore
• Name comes from a creature in Arabian mythology
Morocco
N
W
E
S
Rugops
• Theropod
• Late Cretaceous
• Carnivore
• Very short, useless arms
17

Elliot Formation

The Elliot Formation in South Africa is special. This is because one of the first dinosaurs to be named was dug up there.

Sir
Richard Owen

Massospondylus
• Sauropod
• Early Jurassic
• Herbivore
• Discovered in 1854 by English paleontologist Sir Richard Owen

N
W   E
S
South
Africa

19

Small ornithopods have
been discovered there too.
Pegomastax was just 2 feet
(60 cm) from head to tail.

Pegomastax
Ornithopod
Early Jurassic
Herbivore
Name means "Strong jaw"
Pegomastax lower jaw

Some Major Dinosaur Groups

Ornithischia

Ankylosauria
- Four-legged
- Heavily armored
- Tank-like
- Some members had clubbed tails
- Herbivores

Ceratopsia
- Four-legged
- Solidly built
- Enormous skulls
- Long horns
- Sharp beaks
- Herbivores

Ornithopoda
- Two-legged
- Beaked
- Had cheek teeth
- Herbivores

Stegosauria
- Four-legged
- Small heads
- Heavy, bony plates with sharp spikes down the backbone
- Herbivores

Saurichia

Sauropoda
- Four-legged
- Very large
- Long necks and tails
- Small heads
- Herbivores

Theropoda
- Two-legged
- From small and delicate to very large in size
- Small arms
- Carnivores and omnivores

Glossary

carnivore – an animal that eats other animals.

herbivore – an animal that feeds only on plants.

omnivore – an animal that eats both plants and other animals.

paleontologist – a scientist that studies animal and plant fossils for information about life in the past.

partial – not complete.

Pterosaur – a flying reptile that lived alongside dinosaurs. Had a birdlike beak and wings.

quarry – a large open hole or pit dug for mining.

rock formation – a large body of rock that has a consistent set of physical characteristics that make it stand out from other bodies of rock nearby.

Index

Abdo Kids ONLINE

FREE! ONLINE MULTIMEDIA RESOURCES

Visit **abdokids.com** to access crafts, games, videos, and more!